Alaska

Canada

Aleutian Islands

Hawaiian Islands (US)

Pearl Harbor

*PACIFIC OCEAN*

Mexico

Samoa (US)

Tahiti (Fr.)

Tonga (Br.)

Furthest Limits of
Japanese Conquests

# Series 117

This is a Ladybird Expert book, one of a series of titles for an adult readership. Written by some of the leading lights and outstanding communicators in their fields and published by one of the most trusted and well-loved names in books, the Ladybird Expert series provides clear, accessible and authoritative introductions, informed by expert opinion, to key subjects drawn from science, history and culture.

*The Publisher would like to thank the following for the illustrative references for this book:*
Page 9: Corbis via Getty; pages 11 & 33: Wikimedia Commons; page 37: AP Photo / Joe Rosenthal

Every effort has been made to ensure images are correctly attributed; however, if any omission or error has been made, please notify the Publisher for correction in future editions.

PENGUIN MICHAEL JOSEPH

UK | USA | Canada | Ireland | Australia
India | New Zealand | South Africa

Penguin Michael Joseph is part of the Penguin Random House group of companies
whose addresses can be found at global.penguinrandomhouse.com

 Penguin
Random House
UK

First published 2023
001

Text copyright © James Holland, 2023

All images copyright © Ladybird Books Ltd, 2023

The moral right of the author has been asserted

Printed in Italy by L.E.G.O. S.p.A.

The authorized representative in the EEA is Penguin Random House Ireland,
Morrison Chambers, 32 Nassau Street, Dublin D02 YH68

A CIP catalogue record for this book is available from the British Library

ISBN: 978–0–718–18729–3

www.greenpenguin.co.uk

# Victory Against Japan 1944–1945

James Holland

With illustrations by
Keith Burns

Ladybird Books Ltd, London

On 20 June 1943, the US submarine *Jack* was on its first operational patrol, moving south of the Japanese main islands, when its crew spotted a large enemy vessel. Manoeuvring the submarine into position, the skipper, Lieutenant-Commander Tommy Dykers, gave the order to fire. The first torpedo appeared to be running on a perfect course when suddenly it exploded early.

'Our worst fears about the magnetic exploders were realized,' noted Lieutenant Jim Calvert, the fourth officer. 'After all this training, after coming halfway around the world to get here, our first shot was a premature.'

Fortunately for *Jack* and her crew, they managed to safely escape a vigorous search for them by the Japanese, and later on that first patrol managed to hit and sink three other vessels. Despite this, for the US Navy's submarine fleet, the rest of the year was fraught with ongoing problems with their torpedoes. In all, the US submarines managed to sink 335 Japanese ships in 1943, amounting to 1.5 million tons, a sixth of what the Allies lost in the Atlantic that same year and not enough to cripple Japanese supplies.

It was a source of great frustration to the American crews but also to Admiral Ernest J. King, the Commander-in-Chief of the US Fleet and Chief of Naval Operations. King, one of the most senior commanders in the United States and the Allied Joint Chiefs of Staff, was not much interested in the war in Europe and had been doing his best to ensure the 'Germany first' strategy applied to as small a degree as possible. For Admiral King, there was only one mission in his life, and that was to beat the Japanese as quickly and completely as possible.

At Allied strategy conferences that year, King won backing for his plan to defeat Japan by focusing, above all, on the enemy's sea lanes. A glance at the map demonstrated the sense of this approach. Japan's empire covered a truly vast area: great tracts of China, Indochina, Singapore, Malaya, Burma, the Dutch East Indies, the Philippines, Borneo and New Guinea, as well as a raft of islands in the Central Pacific. All these places involved vast numbers of ant-lines of ships between Japan and their new empire and required manning with troops, arms and supplies. The entire empire was linked by these vital sea lanes. Without them, Japan would be finished.

There were, however, other, competing plans. General Douglas MacArthur, Supreme Commander of Allied Forces in the South-West Pacific, was anxious to retake the Philippines as soon as possible, a former US possession lost to the Japanese. 'I shall return,' he had promised when he left on 12 March 1942. Nothing that had happened since had made him waver from this vow. The British were also trying to protect north-east India and retake Burma. Increasingly large numbers of British-Indian forces were strung out along the northern Burmese border.

What was troubling both American and British war leaders and planners, however, was that despite some successes, most notably in the South Pacific, the map had changed little since those first Japanese strikes nearly two years earlier. And time was marching on. The war needed to be won.

None the less, 1944 dawned with the US Navy, at any rate, in a strong position, with a huge numerical advantage in warships as well as naval supply ships. The torpedo problems had been resolved and US cryptanalysts had made big breakthroughs in cracking Japanese naval radio codes. Admiral King had reason to feel confident.

The war in Europe might have begun in September 1939 but Japan's war had begun two years earlier. Japanese forces had defeated the numerically superior Chinese Nationalists, taking first Shanghai and then Nanking, before capturing giant swathes of eastern China's seaboard and interior. Occupation did not bring the Japanese the riches they had hoped, however. Rather, it sucked up 45 per cent of the army and incurred immense costs, while in the mass of China where Japan had not ventured, the Nationalists under the command of the totalitarian General Chiang Kai-Shek, and the Communists in the north, continued to offer resistance. It was for this reason that Japan, war weary and running short of supplies, began looking elsewhere back in 1941. Indochina, Malaya, Burma and the Dutch East Indies were far richer in resources than the vast expanse of inland China.

Yet while the Nationalists managed to keep their war effort afloat from their new capital in Chongqing, they were in no position to fight back against the occupiers, who ruled the central eastern part of China with unremitting cruelty and savagery. The Japanese regarded themselves as racially and manifestly superior, employed millions of Chinese as slave labourers and beat and beheaded thousands for the slightest of misdemeanours. Displacement, massacres, starvation and destruction on an unimaginable scale was the fate meted out to the Chinese people.

And although Chiang was the undisputed generalissimo, he was surrounded by sycophantic courtiers, corruption and a country racked by extreme poverty. In the north, meanwhile, were the growing number of Communists under Mao Zedung; only the Japanese prevented full-scale civil war. Organizing this unoccupied part of China, let alone even attempting to modernize it, was simply not possible at this time.

The British were already stretched in terms of men and materiel and also were deeply sceptical that bolstering Chiang's Nationalists would achieve much. However, the United States had high hopes that Chiang's China could become a major force and part of the Grand Alliance fighting the Imperial Japanese. Fired by the idea that one day soon a properly trained, modernized and US-equipped army would begin the fightback against the occupiers, the Americans began sending in massive amounts of cash and supplies.

The Japanese conquest of Burma had severed any direct route into China; undeterred, the Americans began flying these supplies from British-controlled Assam in north-east India, over the Himalayas to Kunming, the nearest base in China. This was a dangerous air route at the mercy of rapidly changing weather conditions, soon renamed 'the Hump'. Even so, by 1944, some 18,000 tons a month were being brought into China by air – a considerable amount and an extraordinary logistical achievement.

By early 1944, however, the Americans had accepted it was unlikely the Chinese Army would ever be good for much. Many of the US funds and supplies had been stolen by Chiang and Chinese warlords, and, with the exception of a small number of troops hand-trained by General Joe Stilwell, the senior US commander at Chiang's court, the Chinese Army remained as poorly trained, ill-equipped and good for little as it had been when the Japanese had first invaded.

So instead, most of the US supplies were diverted to feed the needs of the US Air Force in China. Then, as if to underline the ineffectiveness of the Chinese Nationalist Army, the Japanese launched a new offensive in China for the first time in three years: Operation ICHI-GO.

Since September 1940, Boeing had been developing the B-29 bomber, known as the 'Superfortress'. It had cost a staggering $3 billion, making it the most expensive single weapons system ever built, and had incurred all manner of design problems and setbacks. In early 1944, though, it was almost ready for deployment in the Pacific theatre.

Capable of cruising at nearly 300 mph, it was also the first combat aircraft to be fully pressurized, which meant it could fly higher. It carried ground-mapping radar and one in four had enemy radar detectors. This extraordinary leap into modernity could also comfortably carry 10 tons of bombs – its predecessor, the B-17, could take just two – and had a phenomenal range of 3,200 miles. The plan was to operate these against Japan from southern China.

The Japanese had learned about the Superfortress and quickly realized its significance and from where it was likely to operate. With this in mind, the Japanese high command found the will and arms to launch another offensive in China, driving south to link up with their territories in Indochina (later Vietnam).

Some half a million Japanese troops blazed their way across the mighty Yellow River and on into southern China on a 120-mile front. Despite the United States' two years of ceaseless supplies, the Chinese forces were brushed aside. Some forty Chinese troops were killed for every one Japanese, while hundreds of thousands, if not millions more Chinese people were killed or faced famine and disease as a result of Japan's scorched earth policy.

By the time ICHI-GO finally ended in August 1944, Japan held more total landmass than at any point since the start of the war, despite recent losses elsewhere.

The breadth and depth of the Imperial Japanese Empire was something of an illusion, however. Japan was in fact in a terrible position. The larger the empire, the more men were required to hold that territory and the more supplies were needed, neither of which Japan could afford any longer. Both men and materiel were almost entirely delivered by sea, but by the end of 1943, the US Navy had fixed its problematic torpedoes and was beginning to sink huge numbers of ships. After seven long years of war, the Japanese economy was on its knees – some 80 per cent of its entire economy was devoted to the war effort, but precious few new weapons were arriving and both the civilian population and the armed forces were beginning to run short of everything, not least fuel.

Admiral King was determined that the destruction of Japanese naval power held the key to victory, and could very possibly avoid costly and attritional land campaigns. His priority in 1944 was to ravage Japanese merchant and supply shipping with his submarines and to use the overwhelming superiority in the scale of his surface fleets to try to force the Japanese navy to engage in a decisive battle at sea. To this end, he proposed attacking the islands of the Central Pacific: first the Gilberts, which had already been captured the previous November, and then the Marshalls and the Marianas. Capturing these outposts in the middle of the ocean would not only deny them to the Japanese, it would bring the Allied forces closer to Japan itself.

King found an ally for this strategy in General 'Hap' Arnold, the commander of the US Army Air Force. If China could not be used as a base for his B-29s when they finally became available, then Guam, Saipan and Tinian in the Marianas would do every bit as well.

In fact, capturing these island chains would be preferable, because although establishing airfields and bases in the middle of the Pacific was no easy task, it was nothing like as challenging as operating from China – either logistically or politically. By the spring of 1944, the Americans had finally accepted that Japan would not be defeated by a Chinese, American and Commonwealth coalition based in Asia. Rather, the priority for the Americans would be Admiral King's Pacific strategy. Gradually, the noose would be tightened around Japan until the country could barely breathe at all.

Capturing the Gilberts had proved that amphibious operations using the Navy, Marine Corps and Army needed much better coordination and planning – taking Tarawa had been particularly bruising. However, the United States repeatedly proved during the war just how quick it was at learning lessons. New vehicles, such as tracked, armoured carriers capable of swimming, known as Amtracs, not only delivered troops onto the beaches of Kwajalein in the Marshalls but also offered fire support; they were bristling with cannons, machine-guns and flame-throwers. Kwajalein was captured after four days on 3 February 1944, for the loss of fewer than a thousand casualties and only 182 dead; Betio on the Gilberts had cost 1,000 American dead and 2,300 wounded. In contrast, almost all the 5,000 Japanese defenders on Kwajalein and the 3,000 on neighbouring Roi-Namur were killed.

In fact, the attack on the Marshalls had gone so well that Admiral Chester Nimitz, Pacific Commander-in-Chief, brought forward an assault on the Eniwetok Atoll, the last islands before the major Japanese naval base at Truk, in the Carolines, some 900 miles further west. Eniwetok was another stepping stone, swiftly captured in just five days.

On the same day Eniwetok was assaulted, 17 February, Nimitz also launched the aircraft from nine carriers against Truk in Operation HAILSTONE, attacking the Japanese fleet and installations there. Truk was an important forward base for the Japanese so they responded furiously, albeit largely in vain. US Navy aircraft had vastly improved over the past two years, as had the quality and experience of the pilots. By contrast, Japanese aircraft had barely improved at all, while because of the urgency of their current situation combined with the chronic shortage of fuel, the standard of Japanese Navy pilots had taken a nosedive.

Some 21 Japanese naval vessels were sunk, along with 32 vital merchant ships and more than 250 aircraft, catastrophic losses at this stage of the war. Also destroyed were 17,000 tons of precious fuel. The Americans lost around 40 men and 25 aircraft. Truk might have been a tiny dot in the ocean but it was a vital base the Imperial Japanese Navy were now forced to abandon. The US Navy had taken another leap closer to Japan.

The next US target in the Pacific was the Marianas. Here were Japanese airfields, and the islands were heavily defended by nearly 60,000 troops. US submarines had successfully stemmed the flow of supplies here – more than 30,000 troops had been killed en route by newly efficient American torpedoes – which meant that the defenders were effectively isolated. Their task – and they accepted it – was to defend the islands for as long as they possibly could.

Two Marine Corps Divisions – the 2nd and 4th – along with the Army's 27th Division were landed on Saipan from 15 June 1944. This time, the fighting quickly developed into an attritional bloodbath. The Americans were beginning to learn that the Japanese would mostly sooner die than surrender.

Both King and Nimitz expected – and hoped – that the Japanese Navy would mass their forces for a decisive battle and that was exactly what the new chief in Tokyo, Admiral Toyoda Soemu, ordered. Admiral Ozawa Jisaburo, commander of the First Mobile Fleet, had a reputation for aggressiveness and in the early summer began drawing his forces together from Singapore, Borneo and the Philippines. Just one major victory at sea, the Japanese believed, and perhaps the Americans and their Allies would sue for peace.

The Japanese still had some state-of-the-art warships. Admiral Ozawa's flagship was the carrier *Taiho*, with its armoured flight deck, radar, pioneering engines and array of the latest anti-aircraft weaponry. It had been hustled into service early in 1944 without sufficient working-up by the crew, who, to make matters worse, had been rushed into service too and were undertrained. So sophisticated was the *Taiho* that only the engineering officer knew how to operate the ship. He was hastily made its captain.

The standard of seamanship, once so strong, was replicated throughout the First Mobile Fleet. By contrast, Nimitz's forces were both well trained and by now highly experienced. What's more, Nimitz had overwhelming numbers and three, not one, fleets available. The US Task Force 58 alone had 7 fast battleships, 15 carriers with 891 aircraft, 21 cruisers and 69 destroyers. Admiral Ozawa, by contrast, could amass only 6 battleships, 9 carriers with around 500 aircraft, 13 cruisers and 28 destroyers.

Despite the loss of 17 of 25 submarines before the fleets engaged, Ozawa still ordered carrier aircraft to take off on the morning of 19 June, hoping they might still reignite Japanese hopes.

In a mirror of the decline of the Luftwaffe and the growing strength of Allied air forces, the Japanese naval pilots were slaughtered. In what the Americans called the 'Marianas Turkey Shoot', the Japanese lost 293 aircraft at a cost of only 20 US Hellcats. Later that day, the brand-new *Taiho* was one of two carriers sunk by the increasingly dominant US submarines.

A further light carrier was sunk the following day and a further six warships were damaged before Ozawa ordered his fleet to hurriedly pull away. Although some 38 American pilots and crew were lost on 20 June, the Battle of the Philippine Sea was a resounding victory for the US Navy.

On Saipan, meanwhile, the slaughter continued, providing a grim taste of what was to come. Not only did the Japanese fight to the very last, many of the island's civilians were also caught in the crossfire of Japanese *banzai* charges. Nearing Marpi Point in the north of the island, American troops watched in horror as the surviving Japanese began beheading one another and blowing each other up rather than surrender. More than a thousand civilians also threw themselves off the cliffs and onto the rocks below. The surf turned blood red. If anyone had doubted the fanaticism of the Japanese, the terrible tragedy of Marpi Point and the loss of almost the entire 29,000-strong garrison on Saipan made crystal clear what could be expected until the war was finally over.

Guam and Tinian were the next to be assaulted. Guam had been a US territory before the war and was now home to a Japanese air base. Unsurprisingly, it was once again tenaciously held, with the majority of the 22,500-strong garrison fighting to the death.

All but 252 of the 8,000 troops in Tinian also lost their lives in a battle that took the Americans a week. Guam, more heavily defended, took them three to clear, finally falling to the Americans on 10 August, although the last Japanese troops, unaware of what had happened in the wider world, remained hidden in the hills until they were discovered nearly thirty years later, in 1972. Among the 2,000 American dead was Lieutenant-Colonel Douglas C. McNair, son of General Leslie J. McNair, one of the US Army's wartime architects, who had also been killed just two weeks earlier in Normandy.

While navy engineers, the 'Seabees', hastily began carving out bigger runways and airstrips for the arrival of the B-29s – now within range of Japan itself – the island-hopping continued, this time with a 1st Marine Division assault on tiny Peleliu in the Palau Islands. Although only seven miles long by three, Peleliu had an airfield at its southern end and its capture would not only deny its use to the Japanese but provide another base for the Americans. Even so, it was tiny and there was a good case for simply bypassing the island, which, thanks to the Battle of the Philippine Sea and the work of the US submarines, was now effectively isolated. The 14,000 Japanese troops of the 14th Infantry Division had been sent to Peleliu knowing theirs was a one-way ticket. Whether they were all eventually slaughtered by the Americans or starved to death was not clear, but Major-General William H. Rupertus, a man who had witnessed the Japanese attack on Shanghai in 1937 and had lost his children to disease while there, was determined to go ahead and persuaded his senior commanders. Rupertus reckoned Peleliu would be crushed in just four days.

In fact, although the airfield was swiftly secured, the Japanese, in a change of tactics, retreated to the ants' nest warren of tunnels and bunkers they had created in the Umurbrogol Mountain on the island's narrow northern strip. Almost every Japanese soldier had to be prised out, one by one, and in brutal conditions: in steaming heat and on jagged dried coral. Rupertus lost half his division in this hellish battle before they were withdrawn and replaced by the Army's 81st Division. Peleliu finally fell on 27 November, some ten weeks after the initial assault.

It seemed that the more desperate Japan's situation became, the harder and more determinedly its troops fought. A nightmarish situation had evolved in which Japanese troops seemed hell-bent on fighting to the death rather than surrendering. Now, at Leyte Gulf, off the Philippines, the first *kamikaze* attacks had begun: young pilots, flying aircraft packed with explosives, simply crashed into their targets, killing themselves and taking with them as many Allied lives and ships as possible. Just a few months earlier, both in Europe and in the Pacific, there had been genuine hopes that the war might soon be over. The Japanese defence of Peleliu and the new suicide attacks from the air ensured such hopes were now completely dashed.

While Peleliu became its own self-contained bloody drama, out at sea another big naval battle was brewing. Admiral 'Bull' Halsey, commander of the US Third Fleet, had been launching carrier raids on the Philippines but also on Okinawa and Formosa (now Taiwan), both Japanese home territories. These were a reminder to the Japanese of just how close the Americans now were.

Meanwhile, the Philippines, not Formosa as Admiral King had originally urged, would be the next target for the Allies.

That General MacArthur would be allowed to fulfill his promise of returning to the islands he had left in March 1942 was in part down to Admiral Nimitz's backing. Ever the diplomat, Nimitz was eager to be as cooperative as possible and had assigned Halsey's Third Fleet, which included Australian and New Zealand and even Mexican naval forces, to support MacArthur's operations. And MacArthur was determined that the Philippines, previously his own fiefdom and an American imperial possession, should once more fly the Stars and Stripes without further delay. In this, the Allied Chiefs of Staff acquiesced.

Even Japanese intelligence, often badly flawed, realized this would be the Americans' next move. In Tokyo, Admiral Toyoda decided to throw his surviving warships into battle. With dwindling numbers of warships and drastic shortages of fuel and other supplies, he felt it was a last throw of the dice; a potential victory – however slight the chances – would offset the risk of losing a fleet that was otherwise doomed anyway.

The Americans, on the other hand, by now had vastly superior intelligence and soon had a clear picture of Japanese plans. MacArthur was able to land troops on the east coast of the island of Leyte, in the southern centre of the Philippine archipelago, with the support of Admiral Thomas C. Kinkaid's Seventh Fleet, while Halsey's Third Fleet hunted for the decisive engagement with the Japanese. The need to protect the invasion meant that in the Battle of Leyte Gulf, as it became known, the US Navy was not able to coordinate its actions or concentrate truly overwhelming force quite as well as it might have done. The Allied naval forces also suffered damage both from Japanese land-based aircraft on the Philippines as well as from the first *kamikazes*.

None the less, over four days from 23 to 26 October, the Japanese lost four carriers, three battleships, ten cruisers and nine destroyers, along with a further 10,000 sailors. After fifty years of dominance, the Imperial Japanese Navy was a spent force. There would be no more fleet actions against the Allies in this war. The sheer scale of the US Navy in the Pacific, now increased by the Royal Navy's Pacific Fleet and Commonwealth forces, was simply overwhelming.

US submarines continued to send more and more Japanese ships to the bottom of the sea. Some 3.8 million tons of Japanese supplies were sunk in 1944, of which submarines were responsible for 2.3 million tons. Half the entire Japanese merchant fleet was destroyed, while in all, some 197,000 Japanese troops were killed while in transit across the seas – some thirteen divisions, an entire army's worth. These were catastrophic losses. Japanese conquests in South-East Asia had given them what they needed: access to plentiful supplies of oil, rubber, coal, cotton, timber and other precious resources. But they had not been able to get it to Japan and other places where it was needed. It was the tantalizing paradox of their imperial dream: they had gained the vast pan-Pacific empire of their dreams but were unable to milk its assets or keep it sustained. Its very scale was also its greatest flaw.

In contrast, the United States had shown what could be achieved with the kind of industrialization and exponential growth never before witnessed. It wasn't just the ever-enlargening naval fleets that were overwhelming the Japanese but the even bigger numbers of merchant ships keeping this astonishing effort going. Japanese naval ratings were almost starved while American sailors could drink Coca-Cola and eat ice cream.

After swiftly securing Leyte, MacArthur was determined to strike for Manila, the capital of the Philippines, with an assault on the island of Luzon. The numbers of Japanese troops defending the various atolls and outposts across the Pacific had been necessarily small, but on Luzon there was the entire Fourteenth Army commanded by General Yamashita Tomoyuki, known as the 'Tiger of Malaya' after his lightning victories back in 1942. Yamashita accepted that Luzon could not be held but, as with the defence of Peleliu, was determined to hold out for as long as possible, mainly by retreating into the mountains that ran down the eastern spine of Luzon.

MacArthur planned to attack with two armies of his own, the Sixth under the German-born General Walter Krueger, landing north of Manila, and the Eighth under General Robert L. Eichelberger. Both were extremely able and experienced commanders and their intelligence teams had a very clear picture of Yamashita's strengths and intentions. Despite receiving accurate estimates that Yamashita had more than 230,000 troops on Luzon, MacArthur insisted the figure was only 152,000. The Americans still had enough forces to win the battle – eventually – but MacArthur had willingly underestimated Japanese strength, which led to faulty presumptions and a battle that cost a lot more US blood than should have been necessary.

Even on the approach to Luzon, the US Navy was unprepared for the ferocity of the *kamikaze* attacks. 'At this late stage,' wrote a sailor on HMAS *Australia*, 'after all one had survived, the feeling was: "Not now – please not now!"' A *kamikaze* did hit *Australia*, killing thirty and wounding sixty-four. Fortunately, though, the suicide fliers did not target the warships and the landings went off as planned on 9 January 1945.

*Kamikazes* had sunk twenty-four vessels since the middle of December and damaged many more, and the American admirals were beginning to worry about this cumulative toll. Then, suddenly, the attacks stopped. Unbeknown to the Allies, the Japanese had lost 600 aircraft in a month and there were only 50 left in the Philippines. These were hastily withdrawn, to be saved for the future defence of Okinawa and Formosa.

The fighting on Luzon was predictably grim. The all-important Clark Field air base was captured within a week but MacArthur's hopes of entering Manila in triumph on his birthday, 26 January, were thwarted, for although Yamashita saw no point in a senseless slaughter in Manila, Rear-Admiral Sanji Iwabuchi, who had 16,000 naval servicemen in the city, insisted on fighting to the last. The Imperial Japanese Army and Navy had never made good bedfellows.

The consequence was a bloodbath, in which Japanese troops furiously raped and executed thousands of civilians and in which the Americans were forced to fight for every house, street and suburb. The beautiful old city was largely destroyed. 'Relaxing is impossible,' noted one American infantry officer, 'for uncontrollable muscles tighten and teeth are clenched. The blast of a heavy shell is unforgettable, as is the dud that goes bouncing overhead down a cobblestone street . . . Being bounced in the air and stung by blasted debris gets a trooper counting arms and legs and feeling for blood.'

Only on 3 March was Manila finally in American hands, but the Battle for Luzon still had weeks to run, marked by the dogged resistance of Yamashita's men. Even when starving, they fought on. Japanese troops had resorted to eating bats and cannibalizing the dead. More Japanese soldiers – as well as civilian Filipinos – died of starvation than from American guns.

Admiral King still planned to invade Formosa, but it was a big island and Nimitz was not sure he could assemble the combined forces needed to invade. He suggested instead capturing first Iwo Jima and then Okinawa. Iwo Jima was tiny but had an air base within easy range of southern Japan, while Okinawa, much bigger, had even more obvious advantages. General Hap Arnold, the Air Force commander, favoured these targets too.

With the Americans now within touching distance, Imperial General Headquarters in Tokyo sent veteran units from China and Manchuria to prepare the two islands' defences. Some 21,000 troops were posted to Iwo Jima, a sulphurous island of just eight square miles, 750 miles from Tokyo, and which was dominated by the dormant volcano, Mount Suribachi, at its southern tip. This peak came to house a warren of tunnels and bunkers and covered trenches. General Ushijima Mitsuru made it clear to his men that their task was to fight to the death.

Fifteen minutes after landing on the black gravel beaches on 19 February, murderous Japanese fire rained down on the invasion forces of the 4th and 5th Marine Divisions. Of the 24 marine infantry battalions landed, 17 lost their commanders, either killed or wounded, while one battalion after another was decimated. Marines managed to raise a Stars and Stripes on the summit of Mount Suribachi on 23 February – captured in a photograph that became one of the most iconic of the war – but three more brutal weeks of fighting followed, during which this tiny slab in the middle of the ocean was pounded by millions of shells, napalm, mortars, bullets and grenades. Both on- and offshore, the Americans, unusually, lost more casualties than the defenders. The difference was that only 216 Japanese were taken prisoner.

The war had not stopped in South-East Asia while the Americans were island-hopping and destroying the Japanese maritime power. After annihilating most of the Japanese Fifteenth Army at Imphal and Kohima in the summer of 1944, General Bill Slim's Fourteenth Army pursued the remnants out of North-East India in September. Despite the monsoon and appalling conditions, they kept going, into Burma and across the Chindwin River, one of the main natural obstacles in the north of the country.

In December, Indian troops of Fourteenth Army linked up with General Stilwell's US-trained Chinese troops. A few weeks later, the 'Burma Road' land-link to Kunming was reopened, allowing supplies to flow into China at long last. At this point, Chiang Kai-Shek promptly ordered his divisions back into China. If Slim was to retake Burma, Fourteenth Army would have to do it on its own.

Slim's aim was to destroy the Japanese Burma Area Army and, despite the difficulties of mounting an overland offensive in the remote and incredibly challenging terrain of northern Burma, he planned to confront the enemy in the Shwebo Plain, to the north-west of the mighty Irrawaddy River.

General Hoyotaro Kimura, however, the new Japanese commander in Burma, wanted to draw Slim's army deep into the country, where British lines of supply would become overstretched, and then counter-attack. It was an obvious ploy, but Slim soon came up with an inspired counter-plan. One corps, the 33rd, would cross the Irrawaddy and face the bulk of the Japanese forces near the key city of Mandalay. In secret, however, 4th Corps would advance in a wide loop through the jungle to Meiktila, Kimura's main logistics base, some 70 miles south of Mandalay. And catch the Japanese in a trap.

As a further distraction, a third British corps, including a Commando brigade and two West African divisions, would push south through the Arakan on the west coast. The Arakan operation began in January, part of a complex overall plan in which keeping 4th Corps' advance to Meiktila hidden from the Japanese was vital. Incredibly, through their command of the skies, both to keep enemy aircraft away and to drop supplies to General Frank Messervy's 4th Corps below, the Allies managed to pull off what, on paper at any rate, had seemed logistically impossible. The harnessing of land and air power had reached new levels of operational brilliance.

On 3 March, Meiktila fell in an attack that had achieved complete surprise. Kimura immediately ordered his troops to turn south and retake the town, but first the 17th Indian and then the 5th Indian Division managed to hold firm, whilst weakening Kimura's forces further. With Japanese, not British, supply lines severed, 33rd Corps attacked and took Mandalay on 21 March.

Once again, the Japanese had been decimated and now the road to Rangoon, the capital of Burma and a major port, lay open. Also operating behind Japanese lines were a growing number of Special Operations Executive (SOE) teams, working hand in glove with the Burmese National Army forces under resistance leader Aung San. Harassed by these guerillas and by the Fourteenth Army driving south, Kimura abandoned Rangoon, which was captured on 2 May, just as the monsoon began to fall and threatened to make the roads impassable. Victory had been snatched in the nick of time, and although fighting to the south continued, Slim's multinational force of Indians, Africans, Nepalese and British troops, with the help of the Burmese, had achieved what no one had thought possible.

Although the first B-29 raid had been flown the previous June, against Bangkok in Siam, and Japan first bombed a few weeks later, the full weight of the B-29 bombing campaign seemed to be a long time in coming. Air strips on Saipan and Guam had to be lengthened and asphalted, stores brought in, fuel and ammunition stocks established as well as ground crews and services. Really, it was a miracle that both islands were open for business by the second week of November 1944 and Tinian ready in December.

In the third week of January 1945, Brigadier-General Curtis LeMay, a veteran of the Eighth Air Force in England, arrived in the Marianas to take command of the B-29s. It had initially been planned that bombing would target industry only and be as 'precision' as possible. However, Japanese industry was widely spread, the weather was variable and early B-29 raids had shown that high-altitude daylight raids were simply not very precise at all. Instead, LeMay chose to follow a 'just win' strategy, and relentlessly too. When weather conditions were fair, his bombers would attack from altitude during the day; when the weather was against them, they would attack at lower altitudes by night, when Japanese defences were at their weakest.

He also pursued a policy of using incendiaries filled with napalm and phosphorous, which were devastatingly effective against the densely placed, often wooden buildings in most of Japan's cities.

It was ruthless and brutal. The first mass night-time incendiary raid on Tokyo was on 9/10 March. In that terrible night, over 267,000 buildings burned to the ground and a staggering 83,000 were killed. Once again in this war, it was the civilians who were paying the harshest price.

The subsequent incendiary raids that followed, again on Tokyo but on other Japanese cities besides, reflected the Allies' anger and exasperation at the brutality of the Japanese armed forces and their stubborn insistence on continuing the fight. Americans were still battling on Luzon, for example, while the British were fighting in Burma and the Australians in New Guinea. It had been a very long war.

Meanwhile, in the Pacific, the Americans and their British and Commonwealth allies in the naval campaign launched their invasion of Okinawa, home to 450,000 native Okinawans and a Japanese territory since 1879. The island was the largest in the curling tail of the Ryuku archipelago and only some 320 miles south of Japan. By the spring of 1945, Okinawa was heaving with more than 76,000 Japanese troops of the Thirty-Second Army; it was unthinkable for the Land of the Rising Sun to concede such a jewel, no matter how badly the war was going.

Amassed for this battle was a joint US Army and Marine Corps landing force of around 182,000 troops of the Tenth Army and the US Tenth Fleet and Royal Navy's Pacific Fleet – some 1,457 warships and landing craft in all and a mighty armada.

Invasion day was 1 April 1945 – both Easter Sunday and April Fool's Day – and much to the surprise of many of those American troops coming ashore, they did so peacefully without a shot being fired by the Japanese defenders. If the Marines thought Okinawa was going to be a walkover, though, they were cruelly deceived. Rather, General Ushijima had decided not to contest the beaches, choosing instead to lure the Americans into a belt of well-prepared defences. The next 81 days were to prove the bloodiest single land-air-sea battle of the entire war.

To begin with, the Americans swiftly secured the centre of the island and then, after a tough fight, they cleared the north of the island too. Only then was all hell let loose. The Allied naval forces still off the coast, covering incoming supplies, came under repeated attack by *kamikazes*. In all, 1,500 suicide attacks were made for the Emperor in the seas around Okinawa. During the naval and air battle, 64 US Navy ships were sunk or severely damaged; 5,000 men were killed and a further 7,000 wounded – more casualties than had been suffered in the Pacific in the previous two years. The destroyer *Laffey* was hit by no less than six *kamikazes* and lost half her crew.

On land, the battle developed into a terrible bloody slaughter as the Americans, unimaginatively led by army commander General Simon Bolivar Buckner, ran into the series of defensive lines. Cactus Ridge, Sugar Loaf and Shuri Castle all became scenes of carnage. 'You know what it feels like when two nights in a row you don't get sleep?' said Dick Whitaker, a Marine on Okinawa. 'Put a hundred and one days of that back-to-back, and during that time you're sleeping in a hole every night and anything you do could get you killed, including absolutely nothing. That's what it felt like.'

Every yard of southern Okinawa had to be wrested from the Japanese, who used civilians as human shields for their own attacks. A staggering 200,000 Okinawans were killed – not far off half the population. Not until 22 June was the battle finally over. It was to prove the last battle of the war – and one of the bloodiest. Some 110,000 Japanese troops were killed, at a cost to the Americans of 7,613 dead, 32,000 wounded and a further 26,000 lost to accidents and disease.

The Japanese were beaten. They had lost the war. And yet they simply would not surrender; fighting was still going on in the Philippines and in Borneo, against the Australians. The B-29s continued to bomb Japan, US submarines continued to sink enemy ships, but still the Japanese kept going, fanatically to the death. The Allied planners were braced for an invasion of Japan – set for 1946 – in which they expected more than 2 million would be killed. War weariness and growing frustration at the senselessness of the slaughter was infecting the Allied high command.

But there would be no invasion and the war would not drag on into 1946. Instead, Emperor Hirohito agreed to unconditional surrender on 15 August, following the American decision to use a new and devastating weapon: the atomic bomb.

Britain and the United States had been working on such a weapon for several years, drawing on the pioneering work of nuclear physicists from an array of countries, including that of Germany: scientists who had escaped Nazi Germany and found homes in the US and Britain. While Germany had decided back in July 1942 not to prioritize atomic research, in the USA, the Manhattan Project had been given the green light – and immense funding – in 1943. At Los Alamos in New Mexico, some 120,000 men and women worked round the clock developing a weapon of unprecedented complexity and power.

When it would be ready was not entirely clear. By early 1945, they were close, but not close enough to affect the war against Nazi Germany. Then finally, on 16 July, the first atomic bomb was tested in the New Mexico desert, creating a huge mushroom fireball followed by blinding waves of light and crushing pressure. It was the kind of destructive might that could end the world, not just wars.

The decision to use the bomb on Japan was not taken lightly, but it was believed the Japanese would not readily surrender unconditionally as the Allies had demanded back in January 1943. The city of Hiroshima was chosen because it had some military value yet had remained largely untouched by bombers; there was no point flattening an already flattened city.

The first atomic bomb to be used in anger was dropped on 6 August, destroying much of the city and a significant proportion of the civilian population. Still Japan did not surrender, and so a second bomb was dropped, this time on Nagasaki, on 9 August – actually a secondary target, since bad weather prevented them dropping it on Kokura as planned. Nagasaki, a city of predominantly wooden buildings, was largely wiped from the face of the earth. It remains unclear how many died from the two bombs, but it was an enormous number: at least 130,000 and possibly as many as 225,000, although more had been killed by the B-29 bombing raids.

That same day, the Soviet Union declared war and invaded Japanese-held Manchuria. Still Japanese war leaders were split over whether they should fight on, but while they argued and the United States prepared to drop a third atomic bomb, Emperor Hirohito himself told his military chiefs the war had to end. His message of surrender reached Washington and London on the morning of 10 August. After feverish negotiations within Japan and with the Allies, the surrender was announced on 15 August and formally signed on 2 September. The bloodiest, most terrible war in the world's history was finally over. Some 60 million globally had lost their lives, entire countries had disappeared, a new nuclear age had emerged, and the world would never be the same again.